THE BIG GREEN POETRY MACHINE

The Future Is Ours

Edited By Roseanna Caswell

First published in Great Britain in 2023 by:

YoungWriters®
Est. 1991

Young Writers
Remus House
Coltsfoot Drive
Peterborough
PE2 9BF
Telephone: 01733 890066
Website: www.youngwriters.co.uk

All Rights Reserved
Book Design by Ashley Janson
© Copyright Contributors 2023
Softback ISBN 978-1-80459-592-3

Printed and bound in the UK by BookPrintingUK
Website: www.bookprintinguk.com
YB0544X

FOREWORD

Welcome Reader,

For Young Writers' latest competition The Big Green Poetry Machine, we asked primary school pupils to craft a poem about the world. From nature and environmental issues to exploring their own habitats or those of others around the globe, it provided pupils with the opportunity to share their thoughts and feelings about the world around them.

Here at Young Writers our aim is to encourage creativity in children and to inspire a love of the written word, so it's great to get such an amazing response, with some absolutely fantastic poems. It's important for children to be aware of the world around them and some of the issues we face, but also to celebrate what makes it great! This competition allowed them to express their hopes and fears or simply write about their favourite things. The Big Green Poetry Machine gave them the power of words and the result is a wonderful collection of inspirational and moving poems in a variety of poetic styles.

I'd like to congratulate all the young poets in this anthology; I hope this inspires them to continue with their creative writing.

CONTENTS

Brabins Endowed School, Chipping

Mia Thompson (8)	1
Thea Grace Squires (7)	2
Rocco Terramoccia (8)	3
Evie Howson (7)	4
Fraser (8)	5
Rosa Banks (7)	6
Scarlett Freeman (8)	7
Francesca Higham (9)	8
George Dainty (8)	9

Bracken Leas Primary School, Brackley

Florrie Willmore (9)	10
Francesca Lambie (9)	11
Poppy Payton (8)	12
Martha-Anne Hirons (9)	13
Phoebe Sedman (9)	14
Mia Amphlett (9)	15
Grace Morgan (8)	16

Chetham's School Of Music, Manchester

Shirley Zhong (9)	17
Leanne Chung (10)	18
C L 6	20
Joshua Zhou (11)	22
Zoe L 6 (11)	24
S SR6 (11)	25
G W5 (10)	26
Z L4 (8)	27
Wilfred Bolton-O'Boyle	28

Harmony Yingmei Zhang (10)	29
Jimmy Feng (10)	30
R B6	31
Joanna Moore (9)	32
Fergus (11)	33
Immie Gardiner (10)	34
A L5	35
Selwyn Xiyan Chen (8)	36
Ellis Wan (10)	37
Matilda York (11)	38
April T (10)	39
E W4 (8)	40
Sammi Zhong (10)	41
Gabriel Ali (10)	42
Anderson Graham (9)	43

Chichester Free School, Chichester

Jacob Price-Whelan (10)	44
Sophia D'angiolo (9)	45
Amelia McEvoy (10)	46
Will Metcalfe (9)	47
Maxi Markey (9)	48
Anna Barlow (10) & Mariella Mitchell (10)	49
Freddie Williams (10)	50
Emma Firlotte (9)	51
Elspeth Pascall Wills (9)	52
Finlay Hill (10)	53
Persia Aslani (10)	54
Lucy Osborne (9)	55
Zarchi Siekierzycki (10)	56
Owen Yoko (10)	57
Sofie Nergaard (9)	58
Lexi Milne (10)	59

Ella Eames (9)	60
Jack Harper (9)	61
Mia Evans (10)	62
Baxter Gainsborough (10)	63
Noah Foster (9)	64
Henry Mitchell (10)	65
Jasper Mowling Sene (9)	66
Toby Cath (9) & Ollie	67
Eve Pearce (9)	68
Lexie Williams (9)	69
Isabel Cirss-Jones (10)	70
William Squires (10)	71
Amelia-Rose Lock (10)	72
Leah Grogan (9)	73
Gabriella Tolysz (10)	74
Leo Beresford (9)	75
Libby Duncan (10)	76
Reeva Green (9)	77
Benji Ottley (9)	78
Hannah Wholey (9)	79
Leyton Austin (9)	80
Dylan Russell (9)	81
Jaimee-Leigh Owen (10)	82
Elsie Streeter (10)	83
Freddie Redington-Roe (10)	84
Freddie Paffey (10)	85
Emelia Wakeford (10)	86
Alfie Slade (10)	87
Erin Baker (9)	88
Henry Evans (10)	89

Deenway Montessori School & Unicity College, Reading

Radhiyyah Nabil (8)	90
Abdullah Ashraf Ali (7)	91
Faahima Rahmath Abubacker Siddique (8)	92
Laiba Khalid (8)	93
Mustafa Usman (6)	94
Aisha Fafchamps (7)	95
Hajra Faisal (6)	96
Amaar Akmal (6)	97

Drury Primary School, Drury

Dosbarth Malwens	98
Victoria I-W (10)	101
Lydia Bryce (8)	102
Amelie C	105
Emily T (9)	106
George W (9)	108
Ruby John (8)	110
Amelia Burlingham (9)	112
George C (9)	113
Eva Swingle (8)	114
Noah H	115
Catherine (9)	116
Ava Dean (9)	117
Emily Twigg (9)	118
Seren Barton-Morris (10)	119
Harrison (9)	120
Charlotte Lewin (9)	121
Piper B (9)	122
Amy Oxton (9)	123
Ruby Mutton (9)	124
Jessica Cleary (9)	125
Jayden B	126
Finley B	127

Leafield CE Primary School, Leafield

Amelia Field (11)	128
Kitty Brown (10)	130
Emma Harston (11)	131

Mendham Primary School, Mendham

Tara-Belle George (10)	132
Barbara D (10)	134
Lewis H (11)	137
Lilly W (10)	138
Sophie Hinsley (10)	140
Amy B (9)	142
Jasper Milller (10)	144
Elliott P (10)	146

Brogun R (10)	147
Lola M (11)	148

Ringshall School, Ringshall

Violet Jacques (7)	149
Gurtaj Sidhu (8)	150
Theodora Bakudie (7)	151
Erica Nicholson (11)	152
Roux Williams (8)	153
Jack Harkett (11)	154

St Edward's Royal Free Ecumenical Middle School, Windsor

Alice Flores	155

St George's School Windsor Castle, Windsor

Daisy Hopkins (10)	157
Eleanor Bond (10)	158
Aarohi Kakkar (8)	161
Eloise Alderson (10)	162
Josie Lovesey (10)	164
Toby Isaac (9)	166
Suzanne Kankalil (8)	167
Jennifer Hodgson (9)	168
Millie Cheent (7)	169
Florence Miall (8)	170
Nina Jordan (9)	171
Louise Roux (8)	172
Grace Jackson (7)	173
Harriet Wolahan-Black (8)	174
Savannah Tabares (9)	175
Alexander Bond (8)	176

St Joseph's Primary & Nursery School, Crumlin

Ava Matthews	177
Emily Mulholland (9)	178
Joseph Owens (9)	179
Sophie Rice (8)	180

Kiah McInerney	181
Aoife Kerlin (9)	182
Lucy Campbell	183

St Mary's Catholic Primary School, Newcastle-Under-Lyme

Sabrina Neha (9)	184
Akshita Sani Nair (9)	187
Gab De La Cruz (10)	188
Lola Aimee Clews (10)	189
Riyon Thomas (9)	190
Jeevan Jose (9)	191
Rian Socratice (9)	192

Sydenham Primary School, Sydenham Farm Estate

Isaac C (10)	193
Lily Warsop (11)	194
Keva Windrum (11)	195
Dylan Randhawa (10)	196
Noah Alleyne (10)	197

Turning Point Academy, Ormskirk

Joseph Clarke (10)	198

Warlingham Park School, Chelsham Common

Sophia Newman Masterson (9)	199
Sebastian Wentworth (9)	200
Jesse Shambira (9)	201
Lara Luxman (8)	202
Isobel Roberts (8)	203
Emily Olive (7)	204
Antoine Teixeira (8)	205
Ellis Waterman (9)	206
Henry Simpson (8)	207
Elijah King (8)	208
Charlie Cox (9)	209

THE POEMS

What Are They?

There are not a lot of these animals to be true
You can even see them in the zoo
In a group, they're called a streak
And they're definitely not weak
They're an endangered type of animal, you see
All they want is to be free
They're an animal just like me and you
And they don't usually live in a two
Their baby cubs are so so cute
And they're not mute
You'll be quite amazed
This type of animal needs to be saved
What are they?

Answer: Tigers.

Mia Thompson (8)
Brabins Endowed School, Chipping

Help The Environment

Some animals are in danger
It is scary for me
Sometimes it makes me plainer
Makes me go down on my knee
It makes me run home
Plastic in the ocean
I hide in a dome
It feels like I'm broken

Trees are being cut down
I want to stop them
Sometimes makes me frown
It makes me run inside

We save animals so they don't get killed
I swayed from side to side in the wind
I have a stalk
I have bark
I have a crown
What am I?

Answer: A tree.

Thea Grace Squires (7)
Brabins Endowed School, Chipping

The Environment

The environment is very useful to me and you
Why do you chop down terrific tall trees too?
The ocean says, "While plastic runs through me
It makes me cry."
Why do you want to ruin the animal's home?
Why do you try?
So please don't kill the animals, animals are
Just like people
The world is always equal

This is important because you'll see
Without the environment
The world will end.

Rocco Terramoccia (8)
Brabins Endowed School, Chipping

Looking Out For Our Earth

Frogs pound out of the pond
This is like a magic wand

Octopus swimming in the sea
They can see you and me

Bees are making honey for us
"Please don't kill us, we are good."

Will lions come and chase you?
Who knows? Maybe they do

Tigers are all stripy
Maybe they are not nicey

Red deer prancing around
But we don't pace up and down

This is what we need
Please stop killing these.

Evie Howson (7)
Brabins Endowed School, Chipping

Animals

Beetles, bugs
Scuttle around for slugs
Dolphins dive down for food
So they're in a good mood
Plastic bottles float around
So pollution is found
Meerkats eat insects
So then zookeepers don't inspect
Fireflies dance about inside
So they don't catch me eating flies
Stags lie down in the mud
So their claws don't have blood
Without them, we couldn't stay alive
So you and me couldn't survive.

Fraser (8)
Brabins Endowed School, Chipping

Trees

Tree, tree, I'm a tree
There's not much left of me
I give you life I do
I might not be your favourite brew
But I'm a life assistant
I keep you alive and bring you time
You have committed various crimes
We are very mad
I will get my dad
We will fall if you carry on
In the morning we'll be gone
Help us if you dare
There is no more to spare.

Rosa Banks (7)
Brabins Endowed School, Chipping

Animals

L eopards leap and jump around
E lephants swing their trunks from side to side
O rangutans jump from tree to tree
P olar bears stomp for years and years
A lligators snap their jaws at you
R accoons scuttle to search for food
D ogs are cute but very naughty.

Scarlett Freeman (8)
Brabins Endowed School, Chipping

Nature

Nature is a beautiful thing
Go on, take a closer look
There are streams, rivers and even brooks
Nature is the mother of you, us and me
Let the birds fly and the leaves flow free
We need to look after the animals that live
What would we do without it?
We need to save them... Don't quit.

Francesca Higham (9)
Brabins Endowed School, Chipping

The Tree Poem

The terrific tree is a part of the environment
You can see your footprints from walking by
Don't cry when the world is gone
You are going to cry when animals disappear

We need to stop
Cutting down terrific trees
I believe in you.

George Dainty (8)
Brabins Endowed School, Chipping

Our Choices

O ur decisions really matter
U nbelievable how we are
R esponsible for our world

C are for your home before it's gone
H ow we act is just atrocious
O dds are, we lose our homes
I ncredible what we can do
C are is important in these conditions
E very day we are damaging life
S o please, everyone, do your part.

Florrie Willmore (9)
Bracken Leas Primary School, Brackley

Littering

L ittering is bad for the environment
I f you litter, you make a mess
T ake your rubbish to the bin
T ry not to be wasteful
E veryone deserves a tidy world
R educe your waste!

Francesca Lambie (9)
Bracken Leas Primary School, Brackley

Octopus

O nly three hearts
C old-blooded creatures
T entacle lover
O nly blue blood
P ure ink squirts
U nder the waves, my secrets bloom
S limy skin covers me.

Poppy Payton (8)
Bracken Leas Primary School, Brackley

Monkey

M onkeys swinging from tree to tree
O rangutans are under threat
N aughty and cheeky
K ind and cute
E ating lots of delicious fruit
Y ummy yellow bananas.

Martha-Anne Hirons (9)
Bracken Leas Primary School, Brackley

Earth

E nvironment matters
A nimals are important
R ubbish belongs in the bin
T ogether we can stop pollution
H ere we are to protect, not destroy.

Phoebe Sedman (9)
Bracken Leas Primary School, Brackley

Litter

Do you litter?
If you do
Then big thumbs down from me
There is litter on the benches
And litter in the sea

Why is it there?
Because of your actions
I hope this won't happen again.

Mia Amphlett (9)
Bracken Leas Primary School, Brackley

Koala

K ind and cuddly
O val-shaped nose
A lways on the move
L oud eaters
A ttached constantly to a tree.

Grace Morgan (8)
Bracken Leas Primary School, Brackley

The Wrong Wish

"I wish to be you!" said the dog to the polar bear
"You're so lucky to be out free in the wonderful ocean blue."
"But why?" asked the polar bear to the dog
"The ice gets smaller day by day, there's no room for me and you."
"I wish to be you!" said the dog to the panda
"You're so lucky to be seen and loved by everyone around you."
"But why?" asked the panda to the dog
"Our forests are cut down by the cruel humans that live with you."
"I wish to be you!" said the dog to the koala bear
"You're so lucky to be lovely and cute, surely you aren't endangered too?"
"But why?" asked the koala bear to the dog
"We're starved to death with the food that's left, you're so lucky to be you!"

Shirley Zhong (9)
Chetham's School Of Music, Manchester

Blackness

Hark! My voice is not shrill
Heed! My twigs branched far
Steady and still, my arm reaches out
Billowing clouds grey
Can you see it? Just as I see it?
Can you sense it? Just as I sense it?
Can you taste it? Just as I taste it
This burning defeat?
Fizzing, scorching, boiling, churning up inside of me
Clenched between reality
Never could I have sought a fight
Roots pinning me down, as I stay still as still
Cinders, ashes fall onto my beloved brothers and sisters
Ripped apart from Mother
Alas! 'Twas my sweet Juliet, gone forever
Torn away from me, tossing my heart into the soil
Anger shot to my head, heat reaching my leg
Finally, hide-and-seek was over, and I was found
Trapped and cornered, snakes of red slithered up my bark

Woe was bestowed upon me, and my fate was sealed
My surroundings reflected my soul
The world was falling apart in red, yellow and orange
What was reality coming to?
Defeat was bitter. Smoke engulfed me
As the last fresh air my lips lay upon, I whispered
"O woe, cruel world! Fate, sweet as a scorpion!"
Then... blackness.

Leanne Chung (10)
Chetham's School Of Music, Manchester

White Rhinos

White rhinos are suffering in the darkness of
the world
White rhinos are dying each day and night
Can't you hear the howl and cry from the babies
waiting for their parents?
Little did they know, they won't see them again
You did nothing to stop this guilty feeling inside

As one falls, all fall like a domino piece
You left them there after taking their delicate,
precious horns
Breaking their wish on dying peacefully together
You ignored their screams like an ignorant, cruel
person
Families die, friends die, they all die in pain and
agony

Animals cry like humans do
Animals have feelings like humans too
Animals can kill like humans do
But they don't have power and humans do
Don't hurt us, don't destroy our valuable homes

In front of our eyes, our families are killed
Pain and sadness fill our hearts
Our tears are a rushing river
All we have got now is ourselves
All we have got now is nothing.

C L6
Chetham's School Of Music, Manchester

Help This World

The air once bright and profound
Shared across our land
The silence of the sound
Our mistakes will follow us through the
Sea and sand
We threw them into the sea
Without care or notice
We thought, *how harmful could it be?*

Sliced and turned to shreds
Our homes were soon devoured
"We use wood for our houses."
"What about ours?" we said
Forced to suffer every day
Our tears fell through the ground
Some of us never saw the light of day
Some of us could never hear a sound

We beg for mercy
We can't stay this way

For one simple deed
Like planting a single seed
Could change our day

Now we ask you
With all our might
Help this world
And only then will there be a wonderful sight.

Joshua Zhou (11)
Chetham's School Of Music, Manchester

River Flow

Fish were swimming in the refreshing, cool river
A loving home for innocent aquatic life
It sparkles like a chandelier in the soothing sunlight
Nothing to worry about until...

Plastic came suffocating the creatures
Algae stealing oxygen from the harmless river
Sewage entering without permission
Pollution, an enemy for those who swim in
These waters

The river and fish beg you to help them
Like soldiers, they are fighting for their home
Cries are heard from many others
So, tell me, how we can save them?

Recycling your plastic will help them a lot
Give back clean water to the river
Sewage and plastic will soon be gone
If you help the river's life by doing your part.

Zoe L 6 (11)
Chetham's School Of Music, Manchester

Gone Forever, Why?

G reat animals once existed
O nly until humans came calling
N ow, none can survive
E very bit of pollution constantly destroying

F or dinosaurs, it is too late to save
O nly now do humans look up
R arely is the rainforest not a bin
E very bit of waste is as dangerous as venom
V engeful, the world now recoils in horror
E very minute is a death pit
R arely do we ever look up

W hy don't we just look up?
H ow many more must die?
Y et we rarely even bother to notice. What are we even waiting for?

S SR6 (11)
Chetham's School Of Music, Manchester

Where Am I?

"Where am I?" said the turtle, not seeing a thing
"You're in the ocean. All the plastic is going to choke us
The humans did this to us," said the fish dodging the plastic
"Where am I?" said the koala, looking down from the tree
"Run! The fire is coming towards you, they have done it again
The bonfire is spreading. Quick get down!" said the kangaroo
Running and squeaking for its life
"Where am I?" said the person looking around
"What once was a beautiful place
Is now crying constantly. What have we done?"

G W5 (10)
Chetham's School Of Music, Manchester

A Farm Animal's Wish

"I wish I were like you," said the chicken in the cage to the cow
"But why? I need to make milk for everyone to drink."
"I wish I were like you," said the chicken in the cage to the pig
"But why? I get eaten up for lunch and dinner."
"I wish I were like you," said the chicken in the cage to the sheep
"But why? My babies get chopped up to make lamb!"
"I wish I were like you," said the chicken in the cage to the goat
"But why? My life is no better than yours, not until humans change their ways."

Z L4 (8)
Chetham's School Of Music, Manchester

Me And The Plastic

I went out to the sea today and decided to go for a swim
Something shiny glared at me from my shell
It was a plastic ring
My heart fell to the depths of the ocean
I was strangled by it like a boa constrictor
I tried to get out of the plastic cage consuming me
I heard a voice calling me home
Thoughts of my family wrenched at my heart
I would never see them again
But then, everything went black
It was the end
And that is why we need to change our ways
Or the animals, including us, might not see many more days.

Wilfred Bolton-O'Boyle
Chetham's School Of Music, Manchester

Seasons

Beautiful birds chirp their song
On the branches, they sway
The blossom blooms and insects lay their eggs
Children saving plenty of chocolate, getting ready for Easter

On the beach, people swim
Colourful fish around keep them company
With ice cream vans all over the place
The sunshine spreads a smile

As autumn comes
The leaves turn from green to orange
The cool wind blows
And the animals go and get ready to hibernate

The tree is now bare
Snow gently falls to the ground
Frost delicately stays
It's time to build a snowman.

Harmony Yingmei Zhang (10)
Chetham's School Of Music, Manchester

Penguins

The penguins' habitats are being demolished
The snow is melting, the ice is cracking
Leaving these birds with nothing but sadness
The coast is smothered with plastic
Just because of careless humans
Gradually, the temperature rises
Endangering these vulnerable penguins
The oily ocean is killing all the fish
Starving the ravenous birds
Please help these poor creatures
Save them from extinction
Make this world a better place
Just by recycling your litter.

Jimmy Feng (10)
Chetham's School Of Music, Manchester

We Need To Make A Change

Sea life dying from pollution
We need to make a change
Choking birds, throttling fish
We need to make a change

The sea dyed crimson with blood
We need to make a change
The sea doubts its existence
We need to make a change

Trees crying, trees dying
We need to make a change
Sending plants to their deathbed
We need to make a change

Rainforest, gone, deforestation
We need to make a change
Animals, gone, wildfires raging
We *all* need to make a change!

R B6
Chetham's School Of Music, Manchester

Why?

Why is the world so gloomy?
With all the beautiful trees cut down
Why do the flowers all frown?
With the sun sadly looking down
Why is everyone in the house?
I thought nature was good, not bad
Why do I feel so sad?
All I want is to have lots of fun
Why are my mum and dad cutting down trees?
Am I the only one who doesn't understand?
Why do people hunt down animals and chop
Down trees?
Please stop and answer me
Why?

Joanna Moore (9)
Chetham's School Of Music, Manchester

There's A Mountain Ash

There's a mountain ash
Who has lots of cash
He has a salary
Which is unusual for a tree
If you want some wood
Then I don't think you should
Cos he's a mountain ash
And he'll give you a bash
His real name is Rowan
And you will get him going
If you eat his bright red berries
They're not the same as cherries!
You'll need a bucket quick
As you're going to be sick
So leave this tree be
For the sake of humanity.

Fergus (11)
Chetham's School Of Music, Manchester

The Things We Wish To Come True

Unicorns bouncing on cotton candy clouds
Rainbows like a paint pallet on the sky
Massive forests filled with different animals
But the world isn't that good

The trees are being slaughtered
And nobody's noticing
They're crying for help
And nobody's listening

The wood is like an army waiting to die
Animals are simply survivors from the endless war
And this war is against mankind
We started this. So we will finish it.

Immie Gardiner (10)
Chetham's School Of Music, Manchester

What Am I?

I am like a crystal, shimmering in the light
I am a never-ending ribbon, flowing around
the world
I can be calm like a meditator
I can be dangerous like lightning
A reflection of you is what you will see
As clear as a mirror it will be
Rippling hair on the surface, flowing night and day
I am a home to live in for many creatures
Allowed to go with the flow
Allowed to be free
What am I?

A L5
Chetham's School Of Music, Manchester

What Am I?

I get used on Bonfire night
I get used in fireworks as they shoot across the sky
I am a darkness lighter
I can melt marshmallows
I can be used to cook
I can be made with matches
I am a body burner
I spread if it's dry
I am a home destroyer
I can be used for torches
I get killed with water
I destroy the forest and it wails in pain
What am I?

Answer: Fire.

Selwyn Xiyan Chen (8)
Chetham's School Of Music, Manchester

Forest Ablaze

Smoke rushes towards me
Red flaming lights burst in the distance
Racing the koalas trying to escape
"No!" shouted my friends
"In life, everything has a time to die," I said
The sun's heat wraps around me
My branches shiver in fear
The smoke surrounds me
Darkness approaches
I look around for one last time
My time has come.

Ellis Wan (10)
Chetham's School Of Music, Manchester

Endangered Turtles

Turtles are suffocating
All because of you
Turtles are trapped in nets
And there is no way out

Every day they lie on their bed
And every morning they rest
One more friend finds himself dead
All because of you

Stop hurting them
It's not nice
They live on the Earth just like us
They deserve to be treated like us

Stop pollution.

Matilda York (11)
Chetham's School Of Music, Manchester

The Tiger And The Polar Bear

The tiger
Hunted by men with guns
I run for my life
Under the blood-red sky
The slaughtered tigers lie
Gasping for breath
The air is heavy with death

The polar bear
Ice melting
Sea levels are rising
Struggling to stay on land
Food sources dwindling
No place to call home
Nowhere to raise their young
What will the future hold?

April T (10)
Chetham's School Of Music, Manchester

What Am I?

I am black and white
I love to eat bamboo
I live high up in the misty mountains
People can pay to adopt me
I look cuddly and cute
But people won't stop cutting down my home
Now I'm left with nothing
What am I?

Answer: A panda.

E W4 (8)
Chetham's School Of Music, Manchester

Armour Tiger

Armour tigers are dangerously endangered
They die in their natural habitat
Trees are cut down each year
Just leave them be

They are endangered
Just leave them alone
By the time you get there
They're probably dead.

Sammi Zhong (10)
Chetham's School Of Music, Manchester

Forest

F ire rages through me
O rangutans swing in me
R ocks lie in me
E lk eat tree bark in me
S nails crawl across my floor
T he forests are beautiful, save me.

Gabriel Ali (10)
Chetham's School Of Music, Manchester

Fire

A kennings poem

Marshmallow melter
Tree burner
Ice heater
Forest killer
Animal targeter
Habitat destroyer
Rainer of destruction.

Anderson Graham (9)
Chetham's School Of Music, Manchester

Deadly Volcanoes

D eforestation and animal deaths are mostly caused by humans
E arth is trying to fight back because of what we are doing
A nd this will continue unless we stop this
D on't pollute and destroy our world or Earth will continue
L et Earth destroy our things because we are destroying it
Y ou can help stop this.

V olcanoes are Earth's way of fighting back
O ther ways Earth fights are tsunamis, earthquakes, heatwaves and avalanches
L etting us destroy Earth is cruel
C ruel as anything
A nything
N uclear activity is deadly as well
O minous in
E very way
S top this!

Jacob Price-Whelan (10)
Chichester Free School, Chichester

The Lovely Sea

T errible pollution is affecting our beautiful sea creatures
H eartless people still don't realise how it's affecting our planet
E very creature in the ocean should live a happy and healthy life

L ovely oceans and seas should be treated nicely
O ceans are the beauty of our world
V ery many fish are dying because of climate change
E very creature is suffering because of litter
L ots of fish are upset because of all the pollution
Y es, we must do something

S o please come save the seas
E very animal needs a home
A ll our seas are being destroyed so we need to act now.

Sophia D'angiolo (9)
Chichester Free School, Chichester

Bunny Poem

B unnies are cute
U nbelievably adorable
N o one can change my mind
N ot very loud but not dead silent, you may hate them but to me
I can't resist them
E ver so cute
S o many babies but enough love for them all

A dorable tiny faces look at me innocently
R eliving my childhood as they run down the hall
E xquisite little animals, so tiny and cute

C an explode my heart with their tiny faces
U nder a spell of love for them
T ricking me to give them more treats
E mbrace the time you have with them as they don't last forever.

Amelia McEvoy (10)
Chichester Free School, Chichester

Saving Antarctica

T he Antarctic is a playground for wildlife
H ere it is a feeder for global warming
E xcellent soft snow brings the place to colour

A re you aware of the dangers if we don't act now?
N ow peaceful penguins may enjoy the mountains
T he sun is like an oven, it melts the ice
A re you a climate change fighter?
R ight now the sea levels change every year
C ome to the Antarctic to do some research
T he ice groans when it moves
I ce is just a liquid that can be melted
C ome on, let's fight climate change!

Will Metcalfe (9)
Chichester Free School, Chichester

The Rainforest

T rees as tall as skyscrapers
H ot weather changes the temperature
E xotic plants live in the rainforest

R ain as strong as falling rocks
A ir as fresh as green fresh grass
I ntelligent monkeys swing from vine to vine
N othing is as exotic as a rainforest
F orests are dying
O n every branch of every tree sits a parrot
R ain as wet as the ocean
E xotic air like air conditioning
S ome animals are very scared so stop making air pollution
T he rainforest will die if you keep cutting trees down.

Maxi Markey (9)
Chichester Free School, Chichester

The Majestic Rainforest

R ainforests are beautiful with birds chirping
A mazing creatures, all different shapes and sizes
I ntelligent monkeys swing from branch to branch
N ot enough trees to satisfy humans
F ood for the monkeys, food for the sloths, food for the ants, food for the moths
O ver the trees, under the leaves, there lies a beauty next to me
R ealms of the countless, one-of-a-kind creatures roaring, chirping and giggling
E nvironment around me astonishes me
S treams flow as trees sway
T he forest of trees stretches its arms to reach me.

Anna Barlow (10) & Mariella Mitchell (10)
Chichester Free School, Chichester

The Rainforest

R ain pittering and pattering on the leaves
A lways glistening and shining throughout the trees
I hope I could go to this place one day with lots of secrets that I won't say
N ot to chop down all of the tall majestic trees
F or I will help all of the animals in need
O r if I could plant even more tall trees
R ealms of animals all around us
E verywhere I look they are there
S treams twist and turn as they flow through the land
T reacherous predators hunt and pounce for their prey.

Freddie Williams (10)
Chichester Free School, Chichester

The Ocean

The ocean is a treacherous and dangerous place
Taking out its victims at a pace
As sailors drift astray
Their boats sail away

I have many brothers and sisters all over the world
We are cities for waterborne creatures
We are home to whales, sharks and megalodons and so much more
In places, I have coral armour to protect me

I taunt sailors with the worry of death
I give their bodies to the deepest depths
Sometimes they get discovered
There are so many mysteries to be solved...

Emma Firlotte (9)
Chichester Free School, Chichester

Polar Bears

P owerful polar bears are nearly extinct
O n the beautiful ancient Arctic
L ong live the polar bears
A rctic is a place and home to lots of animals
R unning out of land to live

B eautiful polar bears need a home
E veryone should have a home to live
A re you as heartless as some people?
R unning wind as fast as a cheetah
S ome people don't care, are you one of those people?

Elspeth Pascall Wills (9)
Chichester Free School, Chichester

Deforestation

D estroying animals' homes
E verything at risk
F orests are dying
O nce it's gone, it's gone
R uining animals' lives
E very animal running
S topping to eat food
T omorrow doesn't look good
A nimals will die
T oday we need to do something
I s it going to be too late?
O ne day it might not be there
N ow do something quick!

Finlay Hill (10)
Chichester Free School, Chichester

What Am I ?

You can find me on any street as I am
Very common
I can be domesticated
People sadly don't like me
Well, maybe a few
I was once worshipped
I love breadcrumbs
I have many species including the Arabian Trumpeter
I come in many colours including brown, dark brown, blue, white and many More
I try to stay clean but others think we are vile
I make a cooing sort of sound
What am I?

Answer: A pigeon.

Persia Aslani (10)
Chichester Free School, Chichester

The Beautiful Rainforest

R ain is beautiful, amazing and cool
A bird is flying in the sky, singing
I n the night it shimmers like a star
N ow the birds sing loud and clear
F ar and wide the rainforest goes
O ver the rainforest, the animals look
R ainbow glows as light as they can
E lectric eels spark in the waterbed
S mall animals like to run, hide and play
T all animals like to eat leaves.

Lucy Osborne (9)
Chichester Free School, Chichester

Pollution

P oor animals are in distress
O nly we can save Earth
L ook outside your window and appreciate the nature
L uckily, we still have time to save our planet
U nder the sea, animals are struggling to survive
T yrannosaurus rexes are extinct and so will all the animals be
I am doing all I can
O nce it's gone, it's gone
N ow it's up to you to save our one and only Earth.

Zarchi Siekierzycki (10)
Chichester Free School, Chichester

The Rainfall

T he world's little secrets that never seem to please
H ow the world is beautiful indeed
E at, sleep, wonder about the Earth

R ivers flow as the trees grow
A nd orangutans will never know
I hope for the world to grow
N ights are endless
F ights never should be
A ll around we should have harmony
L ook after our Earth
L ong may it live.

Owen Yoko (10)
Chichester Free School, Chichester

My Marvellous Mustangs

Wild mustangs sprint freely through the long grass
Beats of hooves galloping across
Majestic coats glisten in the early sunlight
Wherever they go the wind will follow
When they jump it looks like they're flying
As they run like they're dancing and prancing
While they trot across the beautiful fjord full of daisies
I wonder if only things like this happen in dreams
Yet I'm wide awake!

Sofie Nergaard (9)
Chichester Free School, Chichester

The Beautiful Sea Life

The endless coral slowly dying
As the lonely light fish are slowly getting weaker

Flapping fish, flying fish, all types of fish
Struggling as the Earth is getting warmer

And more rubbish getting chucked in
As people say, the 'fish-choker'

Sharks can be as strong as two crocodiles combined
Sharks are never wrong, swimming through the sea
As the sea kings and queens.

Lexi Milne (10)
Chichester Free School, Chichester

Elegant Elephants

E normous elephants
L ie in the warm summer sunset
E ager elephants sway in the
P henomenal shimmering orange skies
H armless elephants gulp the crystal-clear lake
A dorable elephants trot in the silent savannah
N oisy elephants chomp on hay and straw
T remendous elephants flap their giant eyelids
S tealthy elephants are the best elephants.

Ella Eames (9)
Chichester Free School, Chichester

Polar Bear

P ollution is destroying their homes
O nly some remain
L onely polar bears at sea
A nd they can't get back
R umbling bellies with no food

B ut we can stop it
E arth is a wonderful place and let's keep it that way
A nd we can stop it
R ead this and stop the abuse
S ee, we can keep something amazing.

Jack Harper (9)
Chichester Free School, Chichester

Save The Ocean

S ave the ocean creatures
A ll around the world
V ery full of plastic
E ndangering the species

T he world is full of plastic
H elp to clean the sea
E veryone get involved

O nly you can help
C an we save the ocean
E veryone join in
A lways help the environment
N ever litter.

Mia Evans (10)
Chichester Free School, Chichester

A Ladybird Poem

L uscious ladybirds fly through the air
A bug with jet-black dots
D ots on her militant red wings
Y ou can hardly see them because they're so small
B ut they can be some animals' dinner
I can't see them anymore
R oosters also eat them
D ots are disappearing
S o that's why we need to save the ladybirds.

Baxter Gainsborough (10)
Chichester Free School, Chichester

The Rainforest

R ainbows call, let's come out
A nts carry food on their back
I ndigo plants might be poisonous
N ever say never in the forest
F rogs jump high, higher than me
O ctopus, no, no, not here
R oaring animals have a fight
E lectric eels give you a shock
S hould you be careful
T he vicious is waiting.

Noah Foster (9)
Chichester Free School, Chichester

What Am I?

As the curtain of night falls
Elegant leaves form
I dance alone
Hoping for somewhat company
Small scaly fish swim in me
Lush reefs are surrounded
By all kinds of fish and jagged rocks
Old sunken ships crumble
Like the environment around them
Due to global warming
I am dying, just like all things do
What am I?

Answer: The sea.

Henry Mitchell (10)
Chichester Free School, Chichester

Ocean Life

O cean is the fishes' guardian
C rashing against the steep cliffs
E legant fish swimming inside it
A nimals of all shapes and sizes
N othing is more beautiful

L ovely ocean
I t almost looks like it's waving
F abulous sharks gliding across the ocean
E nough of rubbish in the ocean.

Jasper Mowling Sene (9)
Chichester Free School, Chichester

Rainforests

Rainforests are amazing
Sadly, a lot are in danger
There are trees like soldiers
It's a colourful place
But there are huge machines turning it into a state
Animals getting killed like they're getting eaten
On a plate
My favourite place is getting deforested too quick
We must save it before it's too late!

Toby Cath (9) & Ollie
Chichester Free School, Chichester

The Beauty Of Horses

In the beautiful countryside
There live the most amazing animals
But one is the best, horses and ponies
They run freely, as free as a butterfly
They gallop, they canter, they trot, they walk
They're so amazing, they can do it all
Grass flies into the air as they gallop by
As they stick together in their herd forever.

Eve Pearce (9)
Chichester Free School, Chichester

What Am I?

I swim from sea to sea
Playing together happily
Make sure you don't invade my place
Otherwise, I'll think you're from outer space

I elegantly swim underwater
People think I might slaughter
From time to time, I cry out loud
Making an amazing sound
What am I?

Answer: A dolphin.

Lexie Williams (9)
Chichester Free School, Chichester

What Am I?

I've got astonishing animals in me
And I'm one of nature's beauties
I am dying slowly because of people chopping trees down in me
So all my animals are starting to be homeless
Some have been here for ages and are now becoming extinct
What am I?

Answer: *The rainforest.*

Isabel Cirss-Jones (10)
Chichester Free School, Chichester

What Am I?

Lots of things live in me
You cool down in me
Usually, you come and visit me in the summer
I can be warm or cold
I can be rough or calm
You look at me and think I'm sweet
But be careful, you might be in for a bit of a treat
What am I?

Answer: The ocean.

William Squires (10)
Chichester Free School, Chichester

Turtle's Life

T urtles swim beneath the ocean
U nderneath the coral reef
R iding along the wave's current
T urtles trying not to be eaten
L ife is hard when sharks are around
E asy riding when food is food
S ave the ocean to save the turtles.

Amelia-Rose Lock (10)
Chichester Free School, Chichester

What Am I?

I have a belly but it doesn't rumble
I have a mouth but I don't speak
I have a bed but don't sleep
The fish swim wildly in my waters
I have a bank but do not take money
I'm always changing and always flowing
What am I?

Answer: A river.

Leah Grogan (9)
Chichester Free School, Chichester

The Rainforest

Orangutans are endangered
We put their houses in danger
They are locked up in cages
They miss the touch of trees
The delicious taste of bugs
Global warming makes it worse
The sun takes the water
The peaceful bird's songs
Are exchanged by the sound of saws.

Gabriella Tolysz (10)
Chichester Free School, Chichester

Nature

N othing more beautiful than nature
A mazing animals across the world
T ough animals such as sharks and whales
U nder the sea with all the shells
R ough shells, smooth shells and even shiny shells
E ndless amazing animals everywhere.

Leo Beresford (9)
Chichester Free School, Chichester

Silly Monkeys!

The monkeys swing from tree to tree
They play together mischievously
They are funny brown mammals
They're together every day
When you go near them they just want to play
They're your happy furry friend
I bet they'll stay with you till the very end!

Libby Duncan (10)
Chichester Free School, Chichester

What Am I?

Animals live in my habitat
I have lots of species
Lots of coral live in my home
I am one of the six biomes
Everyone comes to see my animals
Whales fly through the air
Jellyfish swish through the water
What am I?

Answer: The ocean.

Reeva Green (9)
Chichester Free School, Chichester

Tiger

T eeth are really sharp and strong, you should never touch
I t is bloodthirsty for fresh meat
G reat for strong fighting and for defending
E ager for food and skin to keep on going
R elated to my cat but far more dangerous!

Benji Ottley (9)
Chichester Free School, Chichester

What Am I?

I am dark
I am light
I waddle on a blanket of white dust
I live in the Arctic
I have a beak
My beak is orange
I like to eat fish
I swim in the sea
I protect my baby
What am I?

Answer: A penguin.

Hannah Wholey (9)
Chichester Free School, Chichester

Save The Sea

T he sea is dying
H elp is needed
E very fish will slowly go

S ave it now or it will be ruined forever
E very bit of plastic must go
A nd please help us now before it's destroyed.

Leyton Austin (9)
Chichester Free School, Chichester

Sloths Are Slow Movers

S low movers that move through the trees
L ong branches that I move across
O n the branches sleeping tightly
T op of the trees moving slowly
H igh above the animals, now they can't get me.

Dylan Russell (9)
Chichester Free School, Chichester

Oceans In Danger

O ceans are endangered
C reatures live in them
E very day they're dying
A mazing lives are being lost
N egative emotions are overtaking
S ave the oceans, save them now!

Jaimee-Leigh Owen (10)
Chichester Free School, Chichester

Fires

F lames grow as high as a car
I f you touch me you will burn
R aging heat raced through the black sky
E legant flames are hotter than an oven
S moke flies up into the pitch-black sky.

Elsie Streeter (10)
Chichester Free School, Chichester

What Am I?

I'm small and fluffy, I slip and slide
As much as I jump I still can't fly
Where I swim, it's really cold
And still the shore will not hold
What am I?

Answer: A penguin.

Freddie Redington-Roe (10)
Chichester Free School, Chichester

Bunny

B unnies are so cute
U nbelievably adorable
N atured animals in danger
N ature has been killed by society
Y ou can never change my mind about loving bunnies.

Freddie Paffey (10)
Chichester Free School, Chichester

Koala

K oalas are so cute
O n a long branch lying by themselves
A ustralia is my home
L atest conservation status is that I am vulnerable
A nimalia is my kingdom.

Emelia Wakeford (10)
Chichester Free School, Chichester

Fantastic Tree Frog

F antastic that tree frogs jump almost a metre
R ed eyes
O ily black stripes on its beak
G orgeous tree frogs like sleeping on trees.

Alfie Slade (10)
Chichester Free School, Chichester

What Am I...?

I'm hot
Smoke comes off me
I'm dangerous
I have flames
I burn
Don't touch me
What am I?

Answer: Fire.

Erin Baker (9)
Chichester Free School, Chichester

Frogs

F rogs jumping happily
R ound the tree
O ften
G ross and
S ad.

Henry Evans (10)
Chichester Free School, Chichester

The Green Earth

The green Earth is home
It has everything we need
We hear, see, touch and smell
And everybody loves Earth
It's the only planet with water
There is food and water on Earth
And the food is cool
We should protect Earth and keep it safe
Dogs jump over logs
And tree leaves sway side to side
This is how nature lives its life
Cats chase rats and bats fly in the sky
This is how nature lives its way.

Radhiyyah Nabil (8)
Deenway Montessori School & Unicity College, Reading

Fruit And Vegetables

Potato is a vegetable
Carrot is a vegetable
Tomato is a fruit
All of these are fruit and vegetables
Aubergine is a fruit
Courgette is a fruit
Cucumber is a fruit
Onion is a vegetable
Beetroot is a vegetable
Radish is a vegetable
Strawberry is a fruit
Blueberry is a fruit
Pear is a fruit
Pineapple is a fruit
Raspberry is a fruit
Apple is a fruit
Watermelon is a fruit
I love fruit and vegetables
Don't waste your fruit and vegetables.

Abdullah Ashraf Ali (7)
Deenway Montessori School & Unicity College, Reading

Save The Environment

Every day we walk on earth
We are yelling and telling
But people still don't care
About our environment
Each day it's getting worse
Because people are littering
And don't care that they litter
And even thousands of trees and plants die
So please be cleaner
And let's help to save the Earth
So we are safer and cleaner
Than before so we can protect our planet.

Faahima Rahmath Abubacker Siddique (8)
Deenway Montessori School & Unicity College, Reading

I Love Planet Earth

I love planets
I love to learn about the planets
Earth is the best
I love Earth
Earth is green and blue
And it looks very nice
I love Earth and the planets
Pluto is the smallest
Leaves are green
And they are part of the trees on Earth
I love Earth and the planets.

Laiba Khalid (8)
Deenway Montessori School & Unicity College, Reading

Rainforest

I saw a big tree in the big green rainforest
I went under a big tree in the big green rainforest
I saw a monkey
It was cute and I tried to go closer
I saw a tiger and it made a roaring sound
So I went home
I watched TV about the big green rainforest.

Mustafa Usman (6)
Deenway Montessori School & Unicity College, Reading

Rainforest

It was cool
I walked in the rainforest
The monkey was cute
I walked closer
I saw a lion
It made a sound
I got scared
So I went home
I watched TV
About rainforests.

Aisha Fafchamps (7)
Deenway Montessori School & Unicity College, Reading

Plants

I saw two flowers
It was pink and yellow
I got one and I gave it to my teacher
And then she loved it
She put it in the pot
Then she watered it
And planted more plants.

Hajra Faisal (6)
Deenway Montessori School & Unicity College, Reading

The Big Green Rainforest

I was in the rainforest
I was under a big tree
I saw a monkey on the tree
After seeing the monkey
I saw a snake
Then I saw an elephant
Then I went home.

Amaar Akmal (6)
Deenway Montessori School & Unicity College, Reading

Halloween ABC Poem

A is for alien, confused, scared and shocked. The children ran away in terror to their spaceship

B is for bats. The black bat was in the dark damp cave. I could hear it say, "Follow me, follow me."

C is for cobwebs. Cobwebs in a dark deep cave

D is for Dracula. The dangerous deadly Dracula made a death trap as deadly as a dinosaur

E is for evil. An evil monster that's as tall as a mountain that's as tall as the sky

F is for a frightening feline. The frightening feline was as lucky as a soft green four-leaf clover

G is for a ghost. The deadliest ghost roamed around the spooky, horrible, haunted, horrifying house

H is for a haunted house. The haunted house screamed your name over and over again, persuading you to enter if you dare

I is for in disguise. In disguise, spies instantly fall into an icky situation

J is for Jack-o'-lantern. The terrifying Jack-o'-lantern gave me haunted, horrifying looks

K is for killer bat. The killer bat says goodbye when his fangs reached your skin

L is for a lying zombie. The lying zombie said that bats nearly swept me away into the darkness
M is for milk. We need milk to drink, it comes out of cows
N is for the night. The night sky was as black as a witch's hat
O is for owl. The owl was as loud as a creaking door
P is for a parrot. The broken wings of a parrot flying through a haunted house during Victorian times
Q is for a quiet zombie. The quiet quaking zombie quailed whilst eating a Quorn nugget
R is for raven. The raven was as tall as a house and as long as a field
S is for spooky school. A school is a fun place to play with your friends
T is for a tarantula. The tarantula is as big as a big long tall house
U is for an ugly spider. The ugly spider is as old as a rusty old Tudor house
V is for violence. The violent pumpkin is too violent to handle and has two mummies and five clowns hostage

W is for the wicked witch. The wicked witch was watching you sleep in your bunk beds giving you horrifying horrid nightmares in your head
X is for the xylophone. The xylophone sounded as deadly as can be
Y is for yells! The boy was running away yelling like he was about to get eaten
Z is for zombies. The zombies were digging into my brain.

Dosbarth Malwens
Drury Primary School, Drury

The Arctic

T is for the treacherous, tremendous, terrific sightings in the Arctic
H is for the hunger the animals of the Arctic suffer day after day as their prey is slowly disappearing as this world turns into a disaster
E is for the eco-system that frowns in defeat as its home dies

A is for the illuminating, Aurora Borealis which are like crystals in a cave reflecting everything in its path
R is for the remains of the Arctic animals that are nothing but screaming souls that are filled with anger and sorrow as their land is being destroyed
C is for the cold bad lands who growl at the knowledge of how he's so bland
T is for the tummy-twisting, spine-chilling, tongue-ripping, tormenting disasters of the Arctic
I is for the ignorant people of 1909 who ignored Mathew Henson's achievements
C is for the careless, cruel, citizens who left poor Mathew Henson on his poor bottom in the cold, freezing nights of Baltimore City.

Victoria I-W (10)
Drury Primary School, Drury

Tip Of The Iceberg ABC Poem

A is for a frosty, freezing, Arctic area with cool, frigid animals that have warm, frilly, white coats
B is for, big, black boats that crash into the chunked, chilled, iced icebergs that float around in the hard, crushing waves
C is for the crunching white snow with cold frilly snowflakes that flutter on the snowy cat
D is for the drastic, deserted landscape that never melts because there is no brightly and quietly shining sun
E is for shady, black echoes that circle around the snowy, dark, damp caves with cute white foxes with small white ears
F is for frilly faint foxes that blend into the cold, white, deep snow
G is for the gorgeous mountain where the Grinch lays his grubby, green head
H is for the load, noisy howls that some Arctic wolves make
I is for ice, as you trek through the snowy glacier you can almost imagine skating on the cold thin ice

J is for warm, cosy jumpers that you snuggle with as the snow falls outside
K is for the kite, you wind up your kite as the snowstorm appears
L is for love, as it passes by you can feel the freezing Arctic waves crash against your legs
M is for me. "I am a strong explorer," she said softly
N is for natural Northern Lights that glow in the clear bright sky
O is for on the edge of the Arctic as the explorer explored it himself
P is for the perfect penguin that dives into the cold, frosty air and splashes in the deep blue sea
Q is for the cute, cuddly quale that splashes around in the blue dark waves where the fish play lots of fun games
R is for really dangerous, but they carried on
S is for the snowy scene of snowflakes drifting in the cold, breezy air
T is for the gold glowing tinsel as you wrap it around your smooth neck and dance around in the snow

U is for under the iceberg as you only know yourself
V is for very, "It's very cold," said the child as they stepped inside
W is for big bolting whales that spray through their huge holes
X is for a xylophone that you use to play a warm snowy tune
Y is for yummy yellow bananas that you eat as you trek through the frozen snowy air
Z is for the cold explorers that zip through the freezing tundra.

Lydia Bryce (8)
Drury Primary School, Drury

Arctic Fox

A is for an Arctic fox. Arctic foxes are found in cold places like Europe, Asia, North America, Greenland, and Iceland

R is for relentless, reliable Arctic foxes which help to keep the environment clean by eating other dead animals and rodents

C is for cruel cracking icebergs which fall into the ocean

T is for treacherous, terrifying, Arctic foxes which scare away all the rodents with their big teeth

I is for icy impactable icicles which shine on the icy landmarks and lakes

C is for cracking, glorious glaciers which are very cold

F is for the fantastic foxes which run on the cold and snowy paths

O is for the abundance of owls which nest and fly through the snow

X is for a Xema Sabini. A fork-tailed gull found swimming and plucking items from the water's surface.

Amelie C
Drury Primary School, Drury

Tip Of The Iceberg

A rctic foxes leap and jump to catch their prey
B itter, biting, blue, cold day
C onservation, climate change
D ancing Northern Lights with a wonderful colour range
E xplorers look in wonder at the beautiful eagles
F alling snowflakes dance in the air
G liding, slip-sliding penguins whoosh across the cold, icy, glistening land
H uddling penguins try to keep warm
I cicles drip from the dark, cold, glistening ice caves
J umping flying fish leap and soar above the waves
K ind people try to save the world
L andscapes look like lots of lolly ices
M elting ice caps, drip, drip, splash! into the sea
N arwhals deep diving gracefully
O xen with their big shaggy fur and big horns too
P olar bears roam the white, icy, glistening land that's blue
Q ueen of the winter wonderland is the polar bear

R ibbon seals lounge on the great floating icebergs
S nowy owls swoop silently as quiet as a whisper
T rees sway in the cold, frosty, wintry air
U nbearable, cold, freezing, icy temperatures
V ariety of wildlife and wonders
W alruses bask on the thick floating sheets of ice
X -ray fish, see-through and camouflaged
Y etis secretly roam the icy, glistening, frosty ice caves
Z oo animals from the Arctic are being saved.

Emily T (9)
Drury Primary School, Drury

Tip Of The Iceberg

T he thick-billed murre tweets, after teaching his kids to fly
I cy icicles hanging in Iceland and the nearby islands
P erfect penguins! There are no penguins in Iceland

O rcas roam around the Atlantic Ocean while eating kippers
F ur seals swim frantically whilst getting chased by killer whales

T errifying sabre-toothed tigers died a long time ago
H arry, the harp seal, was trying to teach his kids algebra
E mily the Iceberg travelled all the way to the Caribbean as she was being eaten by a shark

I t was a cold icy day with a freezing frosty breeze
C arl, the swirling tornado, chased after the polar bear like a steam train
E va, the electric eel, always eats early in the Arctic morning

B ruce, the polar bear, bites a big blue whale
E xcited explorers explore the Arctic with epic cameras
R uthless reindeer run around like rabbits eating raisins
G reat big humpback whales eat all the yummy plankton they can see.

George W (9)
Drury Primary School, Drury

Arctic Animals

A is for Arctic wolf, cold and chilly in the frozen Arctic
R is for rabbits. Thick white-coated rabbits out in the frozen tundra
C is for cats. Fierce, ferocious felines roaming around the snow-covered boulders
T is for tundra. Animals out in the snow, standing on top of the frozen tundra
I is for icy cold snow covering the frozen fields of the Arctic
C is for cold snow. Animals walking through the thick cold icy snow

A is for the Arctic fox out in the open, it's gone with a swish of a fluffy white tail
N is for the narwhal's sweet silent call coming from the frozen Arctic Ocean
I is for igloo, building a warm toasty igloo out in the freeze
M is for moose. Moose have great big swirly horns so it's ready to charge

A is for Arctic squirrels scurrying across the frozen floor of the Arctic
L is for a lemming digging a small white tunnel out in the frozen.

Ruby John (8)
Drury Primary School, Drury

Northern Lights

N orthern lights shine like a diamond
O ther animals live in Iceland like penguins
R are animals are slowly going extinct
T he Northern Lights are caused by the sun
H ow they got here nobody knows
E xtinction means when the same animal dies
R ailways are gone in Iceland
N orthern lights fly above us in Iceland

L ovely lights shine brightly
I n Iceland, Icelanders believe in elves
G uinea pigs are only brown and black in Iceland
H ere is a picture of a guinea pig
T here is no McDonald's in Iceland
S taying out in the cold weather in Iceland, you can die.

Amelia Burlingham (9)
Drury Primary School, Drury

Northern Lights

N stands for north as in the north and North Pole
O is for orcas who live in the ocean
R stands for rangers in Canada who have a lot of knowledge
T is for the terrific Titanic
H stands for hares in the Arctic
E is for excellent acceleration when animals accelerate to catch their food
R , really pretty lights
N stands for night-time in the North Pole

L is for Northern Lights
I stands for icy igloo
G is for the country Greenland
H stands for hiking on an icy mountain
T is for the city of Tromso in Norway
S stands for the country Sweden.

George C (9)
Drury Primary School, Drury

The Arctic

A is for Antarctica. In Antarctica, penguins swim all over the Arctic to find food
R is for running, leaping Arctic hares. Arctic hares leap away from predators like Arctic wolves
C is for crying baby penguins. Baby penguins cry for food in the harsh winter
T is for terrified young leopard seals. Young leopard seals are scared to be away from ice shelves because of orcas, which eat them
I is for Igloos on ice shelves. Sometimes you will find igloos with people living on the ice shelves
C is for crazy baby Arctic hares. Crazy baby Arctic hares run around excitedly for their mum and dad.

Eva Swingle (8)
Drury Primary School, Drury

Iceberg

I is for the iceberg that the Titanic crashed into on the 14th of April, 1912

C is for the beautiful Canadian lynx roaming around from the tree line in the Arctic

E is for the dazzling ermine stoat that hides in the beautiful Arctic

B is for the beautiful brown bears who get scared by people that make loud noises by yelling, banging pots and pans or using an air horn

E is for the elks roaming the Antarctic tundra like they own the world

R is for reindeer flying in the air on the night of Christmas Eve

G is for the glaciers that are melting because of climate change.

Noah H
Drury Primary School, Drury

Lion Seal

L is for love, the love the animals bring
I is for iceberg, the giant boat of ice that floats in the water
O is for octopuses which hide under icebergs
N is for the Northern Lights, also known as the Aurora Borealis, the shining lights are very pretty

S is for the snow leopards, the very cold meat eaters
E is for endangered species that live in the Arctic, the poor poor animals
A is for the Arctic, it's very cold and is full of life
L is for lovely Northern Lights that shine bright like a diamond.

Catherine (9)
Drury Primary School, Drury

Arctic Fox

A mazing Arctic fox walked along the icy floor
R acing snow fell as fast as a racing rat going in a pipe
C olourful, lights were so pretty, I couldn't stop looking
T wirly, whirly orcas were like a terrifying tornado
I cy icicles shone phenomenal patterns on the icy lake
C almed, grey husky lay down in the cosy tent

F ascinating warm cup of tea made me smile
O range woolly coat kept me warm like a dog's fur
X eno blast, crystals twinkled in the shiny cave.

Ava Dean (9)
Drury Primary School, Drury

Arctic

A rctic wolves roam the wonderful, beautiful ice lands
R ibbon seals bask on the big sheets of bobbing ice, roaming the open wide sea
C aribou are freezing cold in the white landscape sight
T he temperature is melting the wonderful glistening land, while the huddling penguins cuddle
I cebergs crack, splish splosh splash! While wonderful narwhals deep dive peacefully
C ircle. The Arctic Circle is cold every day, the animals are hunting for their prey.

Emily Twigg (9)
Drury Primary School, Drury

Penguin

I am a big penguin
Black and white
Tall and flimsy
A delightful sight
I cannot fly at all
But I love to swim
I'll waddle to the water
And splash, I'm right in
I'm a little penguin in the sea
All the little fish are chasing me
When I catch my prey, just look at me
I am really, really proud as can be
I climb out
Without a doubt
I head to my family
I clamber out happily
We huddled close together
Against the snow and sleet
Penguins sitting in the pole
Freezing cold body heat.

Seren Barton-Morris (10)
Drury Primary School, Drury

Antarctica

A   is for the freezing-cold Arctic
N   is for the glow of the Northern lights
T   is for the big black Titanic
A   is for the white snow-looking Arctic fox
R   is for the white, red-eyed rabbit
C   is for cold Antarctica
T   is for the sunken Titanic
I   is for the country of Iceland
C   is for the coldest countries on the planet
A   is for the Antarctic penguins that rule the land.

Harrison (9)
Drury Primary School, Drury

Arctic

A rctic shines in the spectacular sun, shining on the Arctic animals
R unning rabbits run as fast as a cheetah catching food for their family
C old curious penguins search day and night for their family
T errible plastic litter affects the Arctic animals
I cicles melt in the winter sun and igloos stay nice and cold for their coming visitors
C aps, also known as ice caps, melt day and night because of climate change.

Charlotte Lewin (9)
Drury Primary School, Drury

The Arctic

A rctic foxes change their fur colour depending on the season
R acing, rushing, roaring reindeer run through the snowy mountains
C old, freezing ice is as cold as liquid nitrogen
T he top of the tall mountains has snow as thick as five baguettes placed on top of each other
I t is a fact that less than 2% of polar bear hunts are successful
C ute, clever, charming dolphins leap in and out of the water.

Piper B (9)
Drury Primary School, Drury

The Arctic

A rctic foxes are white like the snow
R ich vibrant colours glitter and light up the night sky in a display of natural beauty
C rystal-clear water is so beautiful like the sky
T he amazing Arctic is very beautiful just like the Northern Lights in the amazing night sky
I n the Arctic, beautiful animals run around in the thick white snow
C rystal-clear water is so beautiful like the sky.

Amy Oxton (9)
Drury Primary School, Drury

The Aurora

A is for amazing aurora in the Artic
U is for ultra-amazing lights that are in the north
R is for regular Northern Lights are very incredible
O is for obvious ultra-rare lights shining in the crunchy ice
R is for red is very rare in the aurora lights
A is for the amazing animals that live in the Arctic.

Ruby Mutton (9)
Drury Primary School, Drury

Arctic

A rctic fox sleeping in his cave with his fluffy fur to keep him warm
R eindeer dance, reindeer prance, reindeer pull the sleigh
C aribou are tough and strong
T is for the tiny lemmings that jump and play
I is for giant icebergs
C is for the Canadian lynx.

Jessica Cleary (9)
Drury Primary School, Drury

Arctic

A rctic Ocean is near Iceland
R eindeer are in Iceland, population of 5,000
C ander foxes are so dangerous
T he pesigans can really be dangerous in Iceland
I ndian Ocean has the largest great white shark
C an some penguins fly? Yes, they can.

Jayden B
Drury Primary School, Drury

The Arctic

A is for the amazing cold Arctic
R is for flying magic reindeer
C is for frozen cold Canada
T is for turbulent ocean
I is for cold frozen Iceland
C is for the Arctic Circle.

Finley B
Drury Primary School, Drury

We Must Protect Our Planet

We must protect our planet

Raging wildfires
Consuming barren lands
The unforgiving sun burning down
On our remarkable landscapes

Thawing ice shafts
Break out across vast oceans
Great sheets of ice collapsing down
Into our steadily rising sea

Deforestation overtakes our rainforests
The crash of trees on the forest floor
Disturbing habitats
And decreasing precious population

Indestructible rubbish overpowers our world
Plastic waste living on
For many years after us
Polluting our lands and seas

Greenhouse gases
Overwhelm our fresh air
Bellowing fumes
Clog up our atmosphere

If we don't take action now
Our future could be wiped out
It's down to us to make a change
And if everyone does their bit
Then, together, we can do it.

Amelia Field (11)
Leafield CE Primary School, Leafield

Out The Window

I look out the window and what do I see?
I see a remarkable world for you and me
The birds sing with grace
Bees buzz at a calming pace
The ivy dangles from the branches so high
And the fascinating eagles fly in the sky
This world is astonishing and beautiful and free
This is our home
It's here that I'm free
I look out the window and what do I see?
I see a world destroyed for you and me
There are no birds, no ivy, no bees
No eagles, no views to please
Who destroyed all these things?
Who took them away?
We humans got greedy and now we must pay
I look out the window and what do I see?
Let's change this, our future, and help out the planet
The greed, the destruction, the damage, let's ban it.

Kitty Brown (10)
Leafield CE Primary School, Leafield

Our Planet

This world is at stake
We cannot let it break
And it we must nourish
For all to flourish

This is our home
The one that we've known
From the sea to the sky
We can fall down or fly

The world's ice will melt
Like all hope we have felt
The jungles will die
Like the dodo's strong cry

Then humans will fall
Like the key to a door
To a world where every
Small girl and young boy

Will breathe in the air of
A new fresher world
Receiving nourishment and care.

Emma Harston (11)
Leafield CE Primary School, Leafield

The Chareot

This is the story of evolution
Of change and adaptation
Transformation and survival
It started 100 years ago

Two beady white eyes open
Its big feathered wings spread out like no
Other
It let out an ear-breaking scream

Beware! The ravenous tigers are coming!
Quickly fly away!

Flapping, screaming, climbing and diving
The chareot is reunited with its family.

Most chareots have grey feathered wings on top of the pebble-grey scales. Their beak is as strong as a boulder
And their tail as red as blood

Although every so often there is a chareot born
With the reddest tail and the strongest beak
The feathers are the lightest shade of grey you would have ever seen.

As the morning rolls around
The ravenous chareots fly and dive, swoop and soar,
Flutter and swerve
In search of food.

As the blazing hot sun shines down on the top of
The trees
The chareots are basking in the canopy
They are ready to lay their eggs.

Tara-Belle George (10)
Mendham Primary School, Mendham

The Chameleon

This is a story of
Adaptation and
Evolution of survival
And hope it started
100 years ago

It starts to wake up
Two small eyes open
Long tail uncurls
And meanders up the tree

Beware! Terrifying
Predators are about
Quickly, dive into the water!

Swimming, climbing
Hunting, the chameleon
Lurked in the trees

However, every so
Often a chameleon
Is born with scales
As white as snow

The chameleons swim
And glide, climb and
Scurry, lurk and meander
To find its next meal

By morning
The scaly climber
Meanders up a tree
And sleeps in a cupped leaf

Scaly-green
Bright leaves camouflage
The chameleon
White scales
Stand out against
The green leaves

A hungry jaguar
Looks for its meal
Who will he find?
Who will be dinner?
The snow-white chameleon
Makes an effortless dinner
For the jaguar

That night, safe from
Razor teeth, the green chameleons
Wander along the tree trunks
Finding the perfect nest
To lay their eggs.

Barbara D (10)
Mendham Primary School, Mendham

Chameezee

The chameezee is born
The life cycle begins
Of the little chameezee

The chameezee is blonde
When it is born
But as it ages, its fur will turn brown
Its scaly tail grows long
And its furry body protects the little chameezee

The five limbs, its tail the fifth
Are used to swing
Through miraculous trees that tower above
Colour-changing fur camouflaged from predators
Protects the little chameezee

As the night begins the chameezee jumps
Quick, up the tree, *shh!*
Be cautious! Beware!
Predators are about
The chameezee hides, beneath the umbrella leaves
The jungle is the home of the little chameezee.

Lewis H (11)
Mendham Primary School, Mendham

A Slocan

This is a story of something new
Of survival and luck
Of light and dark
It started 1,000 years ago with a small sleepy sloth
The Slocan lies camouflaged in the trees, safe from predators

Swinging, jumping, grabbing
The Slocan plays with its friends in the tree canopy
Nearly all have twelve claws
Long, sharp and dangerous
Despite this
They are sometimes born with sixteen claws as long as your hand

As the sun comes into view
The tired Slocans snooze in their warm tree beds
Chocolate brown, wiry fur coats the Slocan
Stones and rocks notify long, sharp claws
Tall, barked trees beam against soft clingy arms.

A famished jaguar craves food
Who will she spot? Who will she find?
The long-clawed Slocan is easy pickings for ravenous jaguars
In later years, the Slocan has its children
All are born with twelve sharp claws
Great for climbing trees
Apart from one with sixteen claws
It's special from the rest.

Lilly W (10)
Mendham Primary School, Mendham

The Red-Eyed Okapi

As the sun rises
It starts 1,000 years ago
With a red-eyed okapi
It starts with adaption
And evolution

As the red-eyed okapi
Suddenly creeps back to its hidden habitat
Where it made its comfortable home
To live in

The next day
The red-eyed okapi unites with its family
Living a happy life with its brothers and sisters

The red-eyed okapi is as scary as a lion
But moves like a tortoise
It has really good feasts

Then things start to change
People start destroying the loving okapi
There is only a little bit of hope left

A week later the red-eyed okapi slowly starts to
Pass on their talented stealth skills to their children

Most of the red-eyed okapi are still living
Hoping their children will be okay
They still pass on their healthy skills.

Sophie Hinsley (10)
Mendham Primary School, Mendham

The Capuchin

This is the story of
Evolution, of change
And adaptation
Of the capuchin

Suddenly at dawn
It heard something scratching
The capuchin smelt fumes spread across miles
Trees were thickening in black due to pollution

The green anaconda quietly
Slithers up the tree towards the monfro
But
It stops halfway up the canopy
Why you wonder

The capuchin attacked
But sadly, the anaconda
Got most of them
And decided
They would be a lovely snack

Only the survivors are left
They are the ones who will breed
The ones that will be parents and grandparents

Two beady red eyes open
Four sticky paws unfold
Every month
Year by year
This magical time
Happens once again...

Amy B (9)
Mendham Primary School, Mendham

The Snakealotl

This is a story
Of light and dark
Of change and adaption
It begins with ten big eggs
One thousand years ago

One leg escaping from the egg
Then another two, then another three
Until all ten legs unwrap from the large egg

Watch out, a famished eagle
Swooping down from the enormous
Trees up in the canopy, diving
Down for a nice dish that night

The newborn beating and fluttering
Slithering and swerving into
A river out of sight. Who
Will survive? Who will be found?

Soon the rivers go black
And predators can get an
Easy meal. The snakealotls soon
Adapt to be pitch-black like the night sky.

Jasper Milller (10)
Mendham Primary School, Mendham

The Toco Python

What's that?
In the tree top, two fangs pop out, a tail uncurls
A snake with dark green scales, teeth like knife blades

Quick! hide!
A ravenous beast lurking in the deep, green canopy
A bald eagle was pillaging habitats for food
Who'll be eaten?
Who'll survive?

The snake travelled up a tree
And wrapped itself up in the silky, wet leaves
Will he be found?
A couple of centuries passed
A new snake was created...
The Toco Python!

Elliott P (10)
Mendham Primary School, Mendham

The Jathon

In the dark and light cave
Out comes a Jathon
A very special animal in the rainforest
Out steps a green and white furry animal
That feels like a furry, little kitten

They run faster than a leopard
Run, sprint, don't stop
Jump, hop, slope
Stands on top of a tree
They sliver and triver.

Brogun R (10)
Mendham Primary School, Mendham

Ocefroz

It starts with an ocefroz
A small and creepy creature
Peering over the leaves, searching for its prey
His green and black spotted camo cloak
Is his disguise
Hiding in the shadows, waiting to strike
Beware! His hungry stomach is growling for a treat.

Lola M (11)
Mendham Primary School, Mendham

Wildlife Is So Lovely

I looked out of my window
And what did I see?
A beautiful and big bumblebee
The bee was buzzing and smiling
I am sure he wanted to talk and tell me more
"I am a bee and I like to
Take pollen from the flowers, you see
My food is important because without me
You would not enjoy honey
Or my musical buzzing."

Violet Jacques (7)
Ringshall School, Ringshall

Nature Is What We See

Nature is what we see
The hill, the afternoon
Squirrel eclipse
The bumblebee
Nature is heaven
Nature is what we see
Nature is what we can hear
The sea dancing on the shore
Nature is harmony
Nature is what we know
I love to dwell in the forest wild
Where giant pine trees pierce the sky.

Gurtaj Sidhu (8)
Ringshall School, Ringshall

Save Our Oceans

T he ocean is in danger
H elp us be its saviour
E very little thing helps our seas

O ther animals of different species are suffering
C an we save our oceans?
E nd this commotion
A nd stop pollution
N ow
S ave our oceans.

Theodora Bakudie (7)
Ringshall School, Ringshall

Spotted Trout

In the dappled water
There lies a spotted trout
He likes to splash
And play about
Then one day his fin got stuck
Playing in some plastic muck
Pollution was to blame
He wondered what humans gain
From something that stains
The environment.

Erica Nicholson (11)
Ringshall School, Ringshall

Nature

N o one should litter
A nd everybody should recycle
T he world is in danger
U tilise what we already have
R ecycle, reuse and reduce waste
E arth is worth our time, make haste.

Roux Williams (8)
Ringshall School, Ringshall

The Tin Can

I am a tin can
Sat in a van
Hoping not to be thrown in the street
I never disintegrate
I am not biodegradable
As you have a moral code
Do the ethical deed
Throw me in the bin!

Jack Harkett (11)
Ringshall School, Ringshall

The Day Begins...

The day begins...
Up from my bed, mostly like I said
I hear from my parents
"It's time to wake up..."

I head to the table
Trying to stay stable
And smell that delicious smell of my breakfast
But I might want to go to the toilet first...

After that, I have breakfast
With waffles and pancakes
But it never makes my tummy ache...
So I guess that's good!

Then, I brush my teeth
All clean and as white as can be
I also put my school uniform on
And my shoes on my feet.

Soon, I walk to school
But I might want to put my coat on too...

And on the way, I hear a ding
So I have to rush
I meet my friends...

And school begins...

Alice Flores
St Edward's Royal Free Ecumenical Middle School, Windsor

Pollution

Plastic is useful but it doesn't break down
It spends years and years just lying around
It litters our coastline and pollutes our seas
We need to stop using it, you will help, please

Our oceans are full of such beautiful life
But the plastic encountered causes strife
It wraps around their necks, tails and fins
The animals die off and then nobody wins

If we use less plastic then there'll be less in the sea
Our marine life will thrive and live happily
So please use less plastic and think of this rhyme
Let's all save our oceans one piece at a time.

Daisy Hopkins (10)
St George's School Windsor Castle, Windsor

What's Happening?

The Earth is a beautiful blue pearl
In a spacious sea of stars
With its tall mountains and vast seas
We can call this planet ours
The Earth is a wonderful place

Forests of lush green
Oceans of deep blue
A happy planet full of life
I live here and so do you
The Earth is a wonderful place

The Earth is as peaceful as can be
Nothing can destroy it
Nothing can harm it
We're sure it can't. Can it?
Sadly we know the answer

A carbon blanket has wrapped around Earth
Destroying everything beautiful
Trapping the heat and light
And we are to blame for this all
The Earth is a troubled place

Destroying forests
Destroying the sea
Man is heartless and cruel
Doing this is destroying you and me
The Earth is a troubled place

Pollution is ruining Earth
No precious plants
No playful animals
No humans
But there is hope

We are the ones causing the destruction
So we need to fix it
Reduce, reuse, recycle
This will help a little bit
The Earth is a hopeful place

Be friendly to the Earth
Other people will do this too
Create a ripple effect
And the Earth will be safe if you do
The Earth is a hopeful place

Help make the world a better place
Forests free from men
Seas of rippling waves
The Earth will thrive again
The Earth *is* a wonderful place.

Eleanor Bond (10)
St George's School Windsor Castle, Windsor

Nature

N ature smells amazing and is beautiful to see, from the busiest bee up to the tallest tree
A utumn is my third favourite season, it is filled with colourful leaves and bare trees
T rees are green in summer and bare in winter, make sure not to get a splinter
U pcycle more, maybe on a door or perhaps on a floor
R abbits are so fluffy, kind and cute, you can attract them with your flute
E vergreens stay green forever, no matter the season or the weather.

Aarohi Kakkar (8)
St George's School Windsor Castle, Windsor

The World Is A Wonderful Place

Gorgeous glimmering orbs of light
Twinkling sea of stars
Rolling hills of the land
The world is a wonderful place

Thick green forests
With waters of ocean blue
A blanket of love
The world is a beautiful place

The indestructible Earth
Nothing can hurt it
Nothing can break it
Or can it?
The world is perfect

Help is needed!
What used to be luscious seas are now polluted
The lush green trees gone
The world is endangered

Reduce, reuse and recycle they say
We are the cause of the suffering
We are the cause of the life loss
The world needs help

Come join us
Not just for our sake but for the world
I will say this one more time
The world is dying.

Eloise Alderson (10)
St George's School Windsor Castle, Windsor

The World

I am so sad
I am
I am

Animals are dying
Animals
Animals

The Earth is ever-changing
The Earth
The Earth

Every day a leaf drops
Every day
Every day

A new life starts
A new
A new

Trees help us breathe
Trees help
Trees help

We only have one Earth
We only
We only

The seeds we plant make a new life
The seeds
The seeds

Please help the Earth
Please help
Please help.

Josie Lovesey (10)
St George's School Windsor Castle, Windsor

The Boy Who Realised

The wondering waves crash down
As rivers flow with joy
I suddenly pull on a frown
As I look at the TV news

The presenter showed us along
The streams were covered with plastic
I soon thought I was small
I thought that I needed to help

Nobody seemed to be helping
The climate that is now dying
So I became famous
For working hard on issues to do with climate

My name is David Attenborough.

Toby Isaac (9)
St George's School Windsor Castle, Windsor

Flowers!

Bluebells are blue
Snowdrops are white
Dandelions are yellow
Poppies are red
Tulips are pink
In fact, all kinds of colours
Rose are red
Daisies are white
Sunflowers are yellow
Tree leaves are green
But in autumn they are brown
When lots of leaves fall
They make a mess
The eco-warriors will clean it
To make the world clean!

Suzanne Kankalil (8)
St George's School Windsor Castle, Windsor

The World Around Us

We need to learn about the world around us
Especially the sea and how we can help
The creatures need you
When I say you, I mean it

Recycle the plastic
That will be fantastic
All the animals who find your rubbish
Will eat it and go to death

Turn the tap off
Turn the lights off
Turn your computer off
Turn the socket off.

Jennifer Hodgson (9)
St George's School Windsor Castle, Windsor

Nature

N ature is beautiful like a bunch of flowers
A nimals are cute like a smiling baby
T rees are long like snakes, leaves are green like freshly cut grass
U nderground, moles are getting comfortable like people snuggling up in bed
R ivers are long and blue like thrashing waves
E ggs hatch and we see the baby chicks like pop-ups.

Millie Cheent (7)
St George's School Windsor Castle, Windsor

Iceberg

I cebergs are melting
C limate change is warming up the world
E arth is in danger and we are polluting the atmosphere
B urning fossil fuels, cutting down trees and travelling in cars and planes
E veryone is to blame
R ecycle, reuse and go green is the answer
G o and act before it is too late.

Florence Miall (8)
St George's School Windsor Castle, Windsor

Be Eco-Friendly

Grass is green, violets are blue
Rubbish is bad and you know too
You own a litter bin so use it
Stop making our world so urban and be more eco
No one likes a dirty world
Put litter in the bin to stop pollution
Don't let animals lose their habitat because
Of forest fires
Be more eco-friendly.

Nina Jordan (9)
St George's School Windsor Castle, Windsor

Nature Poem

N ature is beautiful
A utumn sees the leaves fall from the tall trees
T rees are amazing and nice to look at
U mbrellas keep you dry from rain and hail
R abbits live in nature and forests too
E lephants are big and tall in the savannah.

Louise Roux (8)
St George's School Windsor Castle, Windsor

Nature

N ature is wonderful
A nd try to save the world each day
T ry your best to be eco-friendly
U se items around your home when being creative
R ivers flow gracefully through the fields
E veryone needs to be on board to save the world.

Grace Jackson (7)
St George's School Windsor Castle, Windsor

My Eco Poem

Beautiful daisies and bluebells grow
On the grassy fields
Recycling, reuse, reduce
Do your part to be eco-friendly
Leaves; green, brown and red, fall swiftly
From the trees
All the animals save in their habitats
Do your part to be eco-friendly.

Harriet Wolahan-Black (8)
St George's School Windsor Castle, Windsor

My Nature Poem

N ature is everywhere
A sea of calm
T he whales are hurt on the outside and inside
U nder their emotions is a broken heart
R educe, reuse and recycle, please
E ven the past still hurts.

Savannah Tabares (9)
St George's School Windsor Castle, Windsor

The Aquatic
A haiku

Dolphins rear and dive
The fish swim in silent seas
Now rising higher.

Alexander Bond (8)
St George's School Windsor Castle, Windsor

Save Earth

S ave the world by picking up litter
A ll around the world
V ery crunchy leaves, up they curled
E very day is another to help the world succeed

E very little detail, every little species and breed
A ll your devices off for sixty minutes
R ound your house, you won't regret it
T hank you for making the planet right
H elp each other to fight, fight, fight.

Ava Matthews
St Joseph's Primary & Nursery School, Crumlin

Dying Roots

I am a tree
My brothers and sisters surrounded me
Then one day a noise arose
My family, falling like dominoes
I saw a blade sharp and quick
Scared to death I couldn't escape
My brothers and sisters
My mother and father
Died beside me as I watched in terror
At last, it left
I was the only one
In a graveyard of trees
It was dreadful being alone.

Emily Mulholland (9)
St Joseph's Primary & Nursery School, Crumlin

Recycle

R ecycle! Recycle
E co council is trying to save our lives
C aring for the Earth and the fish, we love the Earth
Y ou! Help our planet by recycling
C are for the trees, fish and icebergs
L ove our planet
E very day recycle.

Joseph Owens (9)
St Joseph's Primary & Nursery School, Crumlin

Save The Planet

S ee today you can change the world
P eople all around the world try to stop climate change
R educe, reuse and recycle now
I need your help before it is too late
N o one knows how bad it is
G o and carry on recycling.

Sophie Rice (8)
St Joseph's Primary & Nursery School, Crumlin

Roses Are Red

Roses are red, violets are blue
Our earth is dead because of you
Why did you do this?
Our earth used to be perfect
Roses are now dead and violets aren't blue
The earth would be green
But it's grey because of you
It makes me sad to think the earth's not perfect.

Kiah McInerney
St Joseph's Primary & Nursery School, Crumlin

Springtime

S pring is amazing
P eople having fun
R ounding up sheep
I n the spring it is fun
N ow you can go outside
G rowing plants.

Aoife Kerlin (9)
St Joseph's Primary & Nursery School, Crumlin

Spring Poem

S prouting buds
P rancing people
R owing boats
I ncoming bugs
N o more ice
G rowing flowers.

Lucy Campbell
St Joseph's Primary & Nursery School, Crumlin

The Rise Of The Binglebobs

When she broke out of her cocoon
She looked up and saw the moon
It became bright and she saw the sun
And then it shone onto her bum

When she tried to fly up high
She just could reach the sky
Carmelita was still a caterpillar
Slimy, thin, she couldn't believe that was her

However, Carmelita didn't mind
She still felt very fine
She went out every day
And she would joyfully go and play

After playing for a while
Cece noticed a change
She began to notice pollution in the air
Litter everywhere
And when she saw this
She just couldn't bear

All of this slowly began to go insane
And at last her death
A death filled with disdain
A death filled with shame

Suddenly, her body arose
When she went up, her body shone
But she still didn't have wings
Which allowed her to fly
But even without them
She could reach the sky

Carmelita decided to use her powers to make
A speech
About how the world should be
"Together we can be the Binglebob Team
The biggest team humanity (or animality) has
Ever seen
I've suffered death from litter
Yes, I know, how bitter!"
"My sister died from a wedgie!"
Said a person out loud

"Hey, that doesn't rhyme!"
Said another person in the crowd
"Want some slime?"
"Littering is wrong."
"So, it's great if you can come along
We can also change the climate
Believe in yourself, we can do this!"
When she heard cheers in the crowd
Carmelita felt extremely proud

The Binglebobs would increase
And litter on the floor decreased
Thanks to the Binglebob Team
The world at last was at peace
Just how the world should be!

Sabrina Neha (9)
St Mary's Catholic Primary School, Newcastle-Under-Lyme

Environment

E nd of the world is coming soon, so look after the world
N ow or never, the world will be destroyed by us wasting precious things
V ow to care for the world
I n our world, we should work together as a team and save the world
R emember that God created us to look after the world
O ur world should be taken care of by us
N ow we should not litter, stop wasting water and stop pollution
M aking a difference can inspire children to take care of the world
E verybody in the world is equally responsible to preserve the world
N ow today we should follow in Jesus' footsteps and care for the world
T oday we should care for God's planet and people.

Akshita Sani Nair (9)
St Mary's Catholic Primary School, Newcastle-Under-Lyme

I Don't Like Our Forests Burning

It's important to keep Earth green
If it isn't then it's bad
And it's also mean
And the Earth will be sad
You need to recycle
The sea life won't be happy if you don't
And you'll be Earth's worst rival
And there will be consequences you don't want
If you keep Earth polluted
I won't be amused
'Cause I don't like our forests burning
So littering, you better refuse
If not, then that's concerning
So in conclusion
If you smell pollution
And you see litter
There's always a solution
So give the world a filter!

Gab De La Cruz (10)
St Mary's Catholic Primary School, Newcastle-Under-Lyme

Give Care, Love And Respect To Our World

Help save our nature
Why not be a saviour?
We need to help this Earth
And thank God for our birth
We need to recycle
Why not read it in the Bible?
Animals' homes are getting destroyed
That's something that we should avoid

We need to give care, love and respect to
Our world
I think we should be more concerned
The trees are falling
And we just stand back and keep watching
We should try to stop driving cars
Then maybe, one day, we could fly to Mars.

Lola Aimee Clews (10)
St Mary's Catholic Primary School, Newcastle-Under-Lyme

Saving Water And Recycling

We have to save water and recycle more
So we can save the environment
And not waste stuff
We should recycle them or give them to charity
So all of the kids will be happy
We need to be careful so we will help the environment
And have a better environment
We should help all of the people
So they can live like us and have a great family.

Riyon Thomas (9)
St Mary's Catholic Primary School, Newcastle-Under-Lyme

Our Planet

O ur planet should be clean
U nder the ocean is litter
R ubbish is everywhere

P eople should recycle
L egends always clean
A nd if you want to be a legend
N ever litter, but always clean
E arth is a gift from God
T o take care of and not destroy.

Jeevan Jose (9)
St Mary's Catholic Primary School, Newcastle-Under-Lyme

Nature Is Everywhere

Nature is everywhere
Nature is everywhere you go
Everything flourishes in nature
Animals big and small
Plants that grow so tall

Nature is beautiful in every way
Nature is wonderful
So we should say
Thank you for doing your part every day.

Rian Socratice (9)
St Mary's Catholic Primary School, Newcastle-Under-Lyme

Changes

The sun danced on the leaves, making them glisten
The trees were bathed in a warm, friendly light
The clusters of purple blossom hung from the branches
The towering trees glowed in the morning sun, swaying

Suddenly, the green shrivels into brown and the sun fades away
The ground bursts open to reveal snaking ivy, enveloping all the trees
The thorns wriggle and writhe over the ground, strangling the paths
Light changes to darkness, happiness changes to sadness and summer changes to winter.

Isaac C (10)
Sydenham Primary School, Sydenham Farm Estate

Our Ocean

Our ocean is a blessing
But what floats beneath is un-impressing
The fish should be able to breathe free
In their home: the sea

Yet, us humans have other ideas
And we don't hear the ocean's cries
Whilst we are selfish and drop litter
The wildlife think, *how bitter*

So many species go extinct
Now it's time for us to rethink
The world is screaming for a change
So, let's all help to change this littering age!

Lily Warsop (11)
Sydenham Primary School, Sydenham Farm Estate

Nature

She has seen hail crashing to the ground
She has seen other trees not dare make a sound
She has felt a blanket of fog twisting all around her
She has felt a wooden log cracking beneath
Her feet

She has smelt smoke rising from a fire
She has smelt the sweet scent of flowers rising higher and higher
She has heard birds tweeting high in the sky
She has heard chainsaws and her own mind yelling
Why? Why? Why?

Keva Windrum (11)
Sydenham Primary School, Sydenham Farm Estate

My Garden In Summer

It was a very hot day
So, we went to the garden to play
The grass was green
And not a cloud was seen

I went in the pool
To keep myself cool
I ran through the sprinkler
To get myself wrinklier

We had a picnic on the rug
And I was chased by a bug
The lemonade was fizzy
And it made me dizzy

As it was beginning to turn to night
We all lost our appetite
So, we went to bed
And we slept ahead.

Dylan Randhawa (10)
Sydenham Primary School, Sydenham Farm Estate

Our World!

We need to start recycling
Climate change now is frightening
The Earth is our home
Let's not leave it alone

Animals are becoming extinct
If we don't care they will be gone in a blink

Penguins like to hug together
We need to protect them from harmful weather

So, let's protect our environment together
Recycle plastic and share our dreams together.

Noah Alleyne (10)
Sydenham Primary School, Sydenham Farm Estate

Sea Of Anger

In the sea of anger
Where the fish of hate roam
Seals of suffering swim and
The otters of misery dive
The cup lids of doom hunt
And the horrible humans
With the disease spread
Stop!

Joseph Clarke (10)
Turning Point Academy, Ormskirk

Litter

L itter in the sea, litter everywhere
I 'm not very happy that people always do this because it is hurting all the life around us
T elling other people will never ever help because you should always just pick it up yourself
T he creatures on this planet are all being killed and it's all because of all this littering
E verything around us is being destroyed and it's all because of us
R emember everyone to never ever litter.

Sophia Newman Masterson (9)
Warlingham Park School, Chelsham Common

The Wolverine

W olverines are hunters, muscular and strong
O nly on our own because we don't get along
L ive in the forest, open wide
V icious teeth on every side
E very night I rule and eat
R unning around, hunting for meat
I eat lots of berries, rabbits and deer
N orth America, we just love it
E ven though it's really icy we don't like little mice.

Sebastian Wentworth (9)
Warlingham Park School, Chelsham Common

Dinosaurs

D angerous reptiles and creepy birds
I n the rainy jungle, the freezing ocean and the blue skies
N on-stop munching hungrily
O mnivores, carnivores and herbivores
S o you have to be very careful
A nd super quiet
U ntil you sneak past the big carnivorous predator
R apidly tiptoe as fast as you can
S ilently, safely escape the wet jungle.

Jesse Shambira (9)
Warlingham Park School, Chelsham Common

The Ocean

O h, some people think I'm the sea but I'm not. I'm the ocean
C rashing and colliding, I go bumping the sand but sometimes I'm big and scare people
E ating the sand little by little, I make my own sandcastle
A nd I do try hard
N ow I'm rolling, shivering in the winter, impatiently waiting for summer.

Lara Luxman (8)
Warlingham Park School, Chelsham Common

Red Pandas

R ed pandas deserve care
E ven if we can't see them
D on't chop down trees

P lant more trees
A nd don't hurt red pandas
N ature is the best
D efinitely use eco instead of Google
A s you plant a tree every time you
S earch for something.

Isobel Roberts (8)
Warlingham Park School, Chelsham Common

Litter Picking

Mummy and I like to go litter picking
Sometimes prizes we are winning
LitterLotto is the app we use
Picking up litter is something to choose
When we are out, people stop and say,
"Well done!"
We do not mind because it is fun.

Emily Olive (7)
Warlingham Park School, Chelsham Common

The World Of The Future

Turtles dying
People buying plastic every day
Time to stop,
Think a lot
About a better way
Man can help the turtles
By cleaning up the beach
Come on, people
Don't hold back
Our mission is within reach.

Antoine Teixeira (8)
Warlingham Park School, Chelsham Common

Green

G reen means be kind to the environment
R ecycle as much as you can
E nergy needs to be produced renewably
E arth needs our help
N ew ULEZ plans are going to improve our air quality.

Ellis Waterman (9)
Warlingham Park School, Chelsham Common

Never Litter

Don't litter, it hurts the environment
If you then go for retirement
To pick up the rubbish with a litter picker
It hurts the environment so please don't litter.

Henry Simpson (8)
Warlingham Park School, Chelsham Common

About Green Things

You walk on me every day
I appear almost everywhere
I die in winter
I live in the summer
What am I?

Elijah King (8)
Warlingham Park School, Chelsham Common

What Am I?

Rarely brown and white
I am like a bear
I live in the jungle
What am I?

Charlie Cox (9)
Warlingham Park School, Chelsham Common

YOUNG WRITERS INFORMATION

We hope you have enjoyed reading this book – and that you will continue to in the coming years.

If you're the parent or family member of an enthusiastic poet or story writer, do visit our website www.youngwriters.co.uk/subscribe and sign up to receive news, competitions, writing challenges and tips, activities and much, much more! There's lots to keep budding writers motivated!

If you would like to order further copies of this book, or any of our other titles, then please give us a call or order via your online account.

Young Writers
Remus House
Coltsfoot Drive
Peterborough
PE2 9BF
(01733) 890066
info@youngwriters.co.uk

Join in the conversation!
Tips, news, giveaways and much more!

YoungWritersUK YoungWritersCW youngwriterscw

Scan me to watch The Big Green video!